Spotting Malingering

By Daniel Barnett

The Employment Law Library

All books in the Employment Law Library are sent for free to members of the HR Inner Circle.

1. Employee Investigations
2. GDPR for HR Professionals
3. Preventing and Defending Employee Stress Claims
4. Employment Tribunal Time Limits
5. Deconstructing TUPE
6. Changing Terms & Conditions
7. Constructive Dismissal
8. Resolving Grievances
9. HR Hazards
10. Employment Status
11. Spotting Malingering

Published by Employment Law Services Limited, Unit 3, Chequers Farm, Chequers Lane, Watford, Hertfordshire WD25 0LG

Appendix I is an invitation letter based on a version prepared by Acas, and licensed under the Open Government Licence v3.0.
Appendix II is © Information Commissioner's Office, The Employment Practices Code, November 2011, licensed under the Open Government Licence v3.0.

ISBN 978-1-9139250-5-5

Acknowledgments

This is the eleventh book in my series of mini guides on employment law for HR professionals. This one is unusual, as it's not so much content I've created specifically for a book, but instead it's an expanded version of a talk I've given on stage (probably) 30 or more times over the last ten years. So, thank you to everyone who has sat in the audience and asked me questions that, over the years, have found their way into the talk and into this expanded version.

It is also the first book in the Employment Law Library where I have collaborated with another organisation. Psychology Associates is an independent practice of clinicians who are experts in helping businesses increase well-being in the workplace, helping with therapeutic intervention and providing expert reports. Clinical director Dr Kerry Davison reviewed the final version of this manuscript and made significant contributions on the medical aspects, for which I am hugely grateful.

As always, there are a number of other people I want to thank. First and foremost, I'd like to thank Jennie Hargrove for her help with the content. I'd also like to thank Tincuta Moscaliuc for the layout and design, Aaron Gaff for proofreading and Maria Rodriguez for converting the book into the formats needed for Amazon.

Finally, I want to thank the members of the HR Inner Circle for whom I primarily write these small books (and who get them all for free as part of their membership). In particular, I'd like to thank several members who looked at an early manuscript and made suggestions to improve it, namely, Penelope Douglass, Claire Thompson, Sarah Gibbens, Liz Jewer, Janell White, Cheryl Golding, Liz Leathem, Lorna Mapson, Aime Armstrong, Susi O'Brien and Paul Helsby. If you're interested in learning more about HR Inner Circle membership, there is some information at the back of this book.

Daniel Barnett
November 2021

ABOUT THE AUTHOR

Daniel Barnett is a leading employment law barrister practising from Outer Temple Chambers. With 25 years' experience defending public and private sector employers against employment claims, he has represented a Royal Family, several international airlines, FTSE-100 companies and various NHS Trusts and local authorities. Employee clients include David & Victoria Beckham's nanny and Paul Mason (subject of the ITV documentary 'Britain's Fattest Man').

Daniel is a past chair of the Employment Lawyers' Association's publishing committee and electronic services working party. He is the author or co-author of eight books, including the Law Society Handbook on Employment Law (currently in its 8th edition). He is the creator of the Employment Law (UK) mailing list, an email alerter bulletin service sending details of breaking news in employment law three times a week to 30,000 recipients.

Legal directories describe him as 'extremely knowledgeable and [he] can absorb pages of instructions

DANIEL BARNETT
BARRISTER

THE UK'S LEADING YOUTUBE CHANNEL FOR LAW EXPLAINER VIDEOS

WWW.YOUTUBELEGAL.CO.UK

at lightning speed', 'involved in a number of highly contentious matters', 'singled out for his work for large blue-chip companies', 'combination of in-depth legal knowledge, pragmatism, quick response times and approachability', 'inexhaustible', 'tenacious', 'knowledgeable', and 'an excellent advocate'.

He is one of the leading speakers and trainers on the employment law and HR circuit. He has presented seminars for the House of Commons, the BBC, Oxford University, HSBC, Barclays Bank, Ocado, and dozens of other organisations in-house. In 2013, 2014, 2016, and 2019 he designed — and was the sole speaker at — the Employment Law MasterClass national tour.

As well as full-time practice as a barrister and speaker, Daniel is the founder of the HR Inner Circle – a membership club for smart, ambitious HR Professionals. In 2007, he co-founded CPD Webinars Ltd, then the UK's leading webinar training company for lawyers, and sold it to Thomson Reuters in 2011.

Daniel is widely sought after as a commentator in both broadcast and print media on all legal issues. Since 2010 he has presented the Legal Hour on LBC Radio. In 2019, he launched Employment Law Matters, a weekly podcast with short explanations of employment law topics. Subscribe at www.danielbarnett.co.uk/podcast

www.danielbarnett.co.uk
Outer Temple Chambers
Strand, London

How to **BOOST YOUR PROFITS** IN A RECESSION

INTELLIGENT MARKETING for EMPLOYMENT LAWYERS

by DANIEL BARNETT and EUGENIE VERNEY

All employment and HR practitioners are competing for work in a market where clients are more conscious of spend, and competitors from ABSs & large independent consultancies encroach into the market.

In Intelligent Marketing for Employment Lawyers you will discover how the internet can revolutionise the way you do business and generate new clients, as well as increasing fees and obtaining more work from existing clients.

Visit
GO.DANIELBARNETT.COM/BOOKS
for more information.

Contents

Introduction

Employees take the odd day off without thinking much of it, but absence has significant repercussions for employers. It is unsettling, workloads have to be reorganised and colleagues must take up the slack. Morale, harmony and productivity can dip, particularly when employees suspect others of malingering. According to research by office suppliers Viking, employees being untruthful about being sick or exaggerating their symptoms may have cost UK businesses £5.6 billion in 2020.

There can also be serious consequences for employees who are found out. Being untruthful about sickness absence is a disciplinary issue (genuine sickness is capability; fake sickness is conduct). But employers do not always handle these situations well, with some diving in headfirst without getting their facts straight. You need to be inquisitive and methodical, but also cautious, as there are quite a few pitfalls along the way.

If you don't believe an employee is genuinely ill, or you believe they are exaggerating their symptoms, you will find yourself asking questions like:

- Do I believe what they're telling me?

- How much absence is okay? When does it become an issue?

- I think they're swinging the lead, so can I get rid of them?

- Are they really too ill to work, or is it that they can't be bothered?

- What else might be going on that I don't know about?

Most employers won't readily be in a position to really challenge an employee who claims to be too ill or debilitated to do their job. In this book, you will learn how to do just that.

Chapter 1
What is malingering and how do you spot it?

Very few malingering cases are reported in the law reports, or even in the press. That's because, typically, when an employer has strong evidence of malingering, the case will be settled or withdrawn very quickly and, as a result, will never make it to judgment.

Why is malingering important in the context of employment?

First, a finding of malingering undermines a finding of disability. If someone is claiming to be seriously unwell, and you can establish that they are exaggerating their symptoms, it's entirely possible that they will not qualify as 'disabled' under the Equality Act 2010. Therefore, you are not under any duty to make reasonable adjustments or to ensure that you don't treat them less favourably for a reason related to, or arising from, their disability.

Second, malingering is a conduct issue. If an employee is fabricating or exaggerating their illness, it's very likely to amount to gross misconduct justifying immediate dismissal, and there will be no requirement to go through an absence management process or pay notice.

So, what is malingering?

The official definition of malingering is contained in the Diagnostic and Statistical Manual of Mental Disorders ('DSM-V', American Psychiatric Association, 2013) and the International Classification of Diseases and Related Health Problems ('ICD-11', World Health Oganization, 2022). Both are referred to by clinical psychologists and psychiatrists in order to make diagnoses.

Malingering is defined as:

"[...] the intentional production of false or grossly exaggerated physical or psychological symptoms, motivated by external incentives such as avoiding military duty, avoiding work, obtaining financial compensation, evading criminal prosecution or obtaining drugs." (DSM-V)

For our purposes, the relevant incentives are likely to be avoiding work and obtaining financial compensation. Remember, this definition is aimed at clinical psychologists, not GPs or occupational health practitioners.

Frederick D Lipman, an American lawyer, set out four types of malingering:

1. Invention of symptoms

2. Exaggeration of genuine symptoms

3. Perseveration: describing symptoms that once existed, but no longer do

4. Transference: attributing genuine symptoms to a false cause

So, malingering doesn't just mean pretending to be ill when you're not (invention). It can also encompass saying you are in bed with the flu when you just have a mild common cold (exaggeration), or claiming to still suffer the effects of a broken arm when, in fact, it has healed and your cast was removed three weeks ago (perseveration). Or it could be attributing the cause of your stress to your workplace, when in fact it is your home life causing the problems (transference). Invention and exaggeration of symptoms are certainly the types of malingering people would consider most common, but perseveration and transference are (I believe) just as common. Many employers will classify exaggeration or perseveration, perhaps deliberately (and generously) using a euphemism, as laziness.

How to spot malingering

There are some early signs of malingering that employers, HR professionals and lawyers should be aware of:

- an employee who is often ill on a Friday or Monday (or after a Bank Holiday, or before/after any rostered days off), but not at any other time

- an employee who, after being refused annual leave, goes off sick during the same period

- an avid sports fan whose sick days correspond with a big sporting event

- an employee with children who regularly falls ill during school holidays or at the same time each year

- an employee who is ill on days when friends/family/partners are known to be on holiday or celebrating special days

None of these signs mean that the employee is definitely faking their illness. An employee who falls ill repeatedly during school holidays may just be unlucky. The employee's child may bring home germs from school and the employee spending more time with their child may result in the employee being ill. But it is suspicious, and it may be evidence (although not conclusive proof) of malingering.

From a more technical point of view, according to DSM-V, there is an increased possibility of malingering if any combination of the following four criteria is strongly suspected. If two or more of these factors exist, a psychologist should actively investigate malingering.

1. **The medico-legal context of the presentation.** This simply means that the employee has been referred to a clinical psychologist by a lawyer. Normally, people are referred to clinical psychologists by GPs, but if they are referred to a clinical psychologist by a lawyer, that (combined with another factor) is an indicator

of malingering. If someone is referred by a GP, you assume their purpose is to get better. If someone is referred by a lawyer or self-refers while there is ongoing litigation, you generally assume their purpose is to get compensation. There is a big difference between the two.

A marked discrepancy between the employee's assertions when they're being examined and their clinically ascertainable symptoms. If there is a noticeable discrepancy between what the employee says and what the clinical psychologist or the doctor finds on examination, this is another indicator of malingering.

For example:

"Doctor, I can only raise my arm this high." (Patient raises arm a little.)

"How high could you raise it before the accident?"

"Before the accident, I could raise it this high." (Patient raises the same arm higher.)

That is a classic example of a marked discrepancy between what the employee is telling you and what you actually discover on examination.

2. **A lack of cooperation.** I will cover this in more detail in Chapter 4, but it involves an employee being uncooperative during the diagnostic process. If an employee has a genuine illness or injury, it is in their best interests

to cooperate with the doctors and comply
with the prescribed course of treatment.

The presence of an anti-social personality
disorder. Lawyers, HR professionals and employers
can't diagnose anti-social personality disorder. But
psychiatrists can. If someone has been diagnosed
with an anti-social personality disorder (which is very
rare) and at least one of the other three factors exists,
DSM-V encourages clinical psychologists to actively
consider 'illness deception' (the clinical phrase for
malingering).

Malingering to avoid a disciplinary hearing

This is a situation that comes up time and time again.
You invite an employee to a disciplinary hearing and
suddenly they go off sick with stress. Sometimes, it might
be genuine (after all, disciplinary hearings are stressful);
but other times, you'll suspect them of faking it to avoid
the disciplinary process. So, what should you do?

Their GP fit note is likely to say they are not fit to
work. That is not the same as saying they are not fit to
attend a disciplinary hearing. The two are very different
things.

The first step is to contact occupational health. As I
will explore in more detail in Chapter 2, it is important
to ask occupational health the right questions. Ask
occupational health whether the employee is fit
to attend a disciplinary hearing. If you are using a
good, reliable occupational health provider, they are
likely to say yes, they are fit to respond to allegations.

Occupational health might make recommendations for adjustments, or you can just take a sensible approach. There are some simple adaptations you can make to the process, such as conducting the meeting at a neutral venue, doing it over the phone or Zoom, or accepting written representations. It is really important to make sure you have a good, reliable occupational health provider.

Assuming the employee is regarded as fit to participate, you then need to write to them saying just that. Inform the employee that you will consider making reasonable adjustments: they can join the meeting from home, they can provide written representation or they can bring a friend or colleague, but ultimately, the date of the meeting is set and you expect them to attend.

If they then send another GP fit note stating they are not well enough to take part, it won't normally derail the process. As I will explore further in Chapter 2, occupational health 'trumps' a GP. If the employee doesn't turn up for the meeting on the specified date, you give them another chance and arrange another meeting with the same adjustments. If the employee doesn't turn up again, inform them you are giving them a final opportunity to attend at a third meeting, and if they do not attend or send representations, you will make a decision in their absence.

Assuming they don't then attend, make the decision, ensure it is fully reasoned, and write to them explaining your decision and offering a right of appeal.

At that stage, the employee will have had four opportunities to attend and/or respond to the disciplinary allegations (three meetings and the appeal). It is very unlikely that a tribunal will think that you have acted unreasonably in those circumstances. Tribunals are accustomed to employees going off sick with stress when facing a disciplinary, and they are sympathetic to employers in this situation. It is easy to see why employees go off sick in these circumstances. Why would they want to turn up to a meeting at which they know they are likely to be found guilty and dismissed for gross misconduct? Even if the employee is entirely innocent and is simply (and genuinely) anxious about the disciplinary process, and so is deliberately avoiding attending, a tribunal will almost always accept the employer has acted reasonably in pressing ahead when they have offered the employee four opportunities (as described above) to put their case.

On the other hand, if occupational health considers that the employee is genuinely unwell and unfit to attend the disciplinary meeting or respond to allegations, then you have to give them some time. If you are being cautious, I would advise waiting two months and then going back to occupational health for an update. Is the employee now fit to respond to allegations? If yes, proceed as set out above. If no, ask occupational health if there is likely to be a change in their position if you give the employee a bit more time. Occupational health will likely say no, there's not much chance of improvement in the near future. In that case, you should carry on with the disciplinary process, giving the employee all available reasonable adjustments. If occupational health say that they anticipate an improvement in another month, but in another month's time the employee is still unfit to respond; by that stage, you'll have given them three months. If there is still no indication that the employee will be better, or fit to return, you should inform them that you will proceed in their absence and do just that.

Working another job while 'sick'

What if you hear that an employee is working somewhere else while supposedly on sick leave? That may not look good, but it does not mean that their sickness is not genuine. It certainly should not lead to a snap decision to discipline them.

You should take account of whether the employee is specifically prohibited from working elsewhere without your prior approval (either in their employment contract or in a company policy that has been brought to their attention) and whether the work that they are doing breaches that. You should also consider what the work involves. If you employ the employee as a labourer, and they are spotted working on the reception at a hotel, the difference in the physical aspects of the two jobs could explain why they are able to do one and not the other.

Consider mental as well as physical health. Could the employee's second job be beneficial? If you employ them in a high-pressured role and discover they are filling in at a local pottery class while on sick leave, it would not be reasonable to treat that, by itself, as serious misconduct.

Similarly, you may receive reports from employees that the employee who is on sick leave has been posting updates on their social media profiles which appear to contradict or undermine their reasons for absence. Despite your frustration, it's important not to jump to conclusions or make assumptions in these instances. It may be that the activities the employee is engaging in could be helpful to their recovery. In these circumstances, you could address this as part of your welfare or keeping in touch meetings with the employee.

It is important to note and deal with other employees' responses to these types of social media posts as they can become inappropriate and potentially amount to harassment of a genuinely unwell employee. One member of the HR Inner Circle (if you're not a member, have a look at the information at the end of this book) told me an anecdote about once having to deal with a case involving an employee with a brain injury that changed their personality. The employee's whole team decided that she was making it up and started posting unpleasant and unprofessional comments on her social media, leaving notes on her desk and sending her unpleasant emails. They thought she was fair game. They called her 'Princess Fiona' (from the film Shrek), and moved and 'borrowed' her aids such as a special lamp and noise-cancelling headphones. Even if she was making it up, their behaviour was inappropriate and caused real problems.

Of course, there will be situations in which an employee is earning two incomes, and an employer (once it has established the facts) will be within its rights to consider dismissal. The dishonest nature of false or exaggerated sickness goes to the heart of the employment relationship, and in most cases will warrant dismissal after a fair process.

But beware if the employee was working part-time, and is still able to do their second job. That is not always evidence of malingering.

Top tip: You may consider including regular contact obligations within your sickness policy that require the employee (and the employer) to provide updates on any change of situation relating to the illness and the absence. If this was the case, the employee in the high-pressure role that was advised to volunteer at the pottery class should tell the employer this was recommended as part of their recovery or rehabilitation. A failure to report such volunteering might be a factor in a fair dismissal (although, on its own, it would not be enough).

Chapter 2
GP or Occupational Health?

GP

You have no doubt seen plenty of GP fit notes saying, "X is unfit to return to work due to depression/ anxiety." It is important to remember in these circumstances, that if you are an employer, or a lawyer advising employers, the GP is not your friend. A patient can walk into their GP surgery, say, "I'm feeling down and I'm worried about what's happening at work," and the GP is likely to write a fit note saying they are not fit to attend work.

The problem stems from the fact that there is no clinical lie detector test. There is no golden standard, no fool-proof method of finding out whether somebody is telling the truth or not. GPs generally have to take their patients' accounts at face value and believe what they are told. They are used to dealing with disadvantaged people; they see them at their lowest and they have a duty of care to their patients. Doctors also don't want to be sued for negligence. If a GP writes a letter to an employer saying, "I think they're faking it," it is quite possible that that would generate a complaint from the patient about their GP. So sometimes GPs will collude in what is euphemistically called 'illness deception'. They might suspect that a patient is exaggerating, but if they're not certain, they'll often decide the appropriate (or easier) thing to do is to go along with it.

Another problem is that employees can get themselves diagnosed just by looking at a list of symptoms online. If an employee is complaining of anxiety or depression, all they need to do is look up the symptoms, then go to their GP or occupational health and claim to be suffering from those symptoms. It is very easy to do in the age of the Internet. An even more fundamental problem is the screening tools used by GPs and occupational health to help diagnose anxiety or depression. You can read more about these in Chapter 3.

If you are a small business, the cost of occupational health can be a concern, but I really would urge you to find the money for it – it is worth it. If you don't, you may well find that you are stuck paying sick pay for that employee for much longer than necessary (and statutory sick pay is no longer reclaimable from the government, except in limited circumstances where the employee is absent due to COVID-19). In those circumstances, requesting a GP report is better than nothing, but GPs are rarely going to say that their patients are malingering and, often, even carefully prepared questions, are ignored or not answered fully by GPs. Remember that the patient gets to see the GP report and the GP's duty is to their patient, not you.

A member of the HR Inner Circle tells me that when he worked in manufacturing, his organisation had a list of local doctors that they suspected were just churning out GP notes, in some cases without even seeing the employees. The organisation then made a point of questioning all notes GPs issued and the practice soon stopped.

Occupational Health

Occupational health is a safety net for employers. It is a way of getting specific medical information to help you comply with your legal duties and manage the employee's situation. In almost all circumstances, an occupational health report will be better than a GP report, especially in a case of suspected malingering. Generally, you would expect an occupational health report to tell you:

- About any medical condition the employee has and what its effects are

- The likely prognosis and how this will affect the employee's ability to do their job

- Whether or not the employee has a disability

- Whether the employee is fit to return to work and, if so, whether they will be able to do everything their role requires – with or without adjustments

- What should happen next

The key to getting the most out of occupational health is to:

1. Make referrals as early as possible.

2. Ensure referrals are clear, giving all relevant information and asking questions that are precise and carefully thought through.

If you suspect that an employee is malingering, you should put that question to the occupational health practitioner. You should ask them for their opinion on whether or not the employee is malingering. But before you do, make sure you can establish two of the seven pointers to malingering that are discussed in Chapter 4. If you don't, you could be at risk of a constructive dismissal claim.

Remember, the employee is entitled to see the referral letter that you send to occupational health. You can, of course, try using more opaque language. For example, don't say, "Can you tell me if the employee is malingering?" Instead, say something like, "Can you administer any available symptom validity testing?" The occupational health practitioner will be able to read between the lines and know what you are asking for. Symptom validity testing is explored further in Chapter 5.

Just like a GP report, employees are entitled to see the occupational health report. But unlike a GP, the occupational health practitioner will not have a long-term relationship with the employee and does not owe them their primary duty.

The employee might not agree with everything the report says. But whether they are entitled to change it or not depends on what it is they are disputing. Where facts are wrong, these can be corrected. But an employee can't challenge the practitioner's opinions. If the report contains an opinion that the employee is likely to be malingering, that is difficult for the employee to dispute, especially without their own medical evidence (and, as you will see below, an occupational health report 'trumps' a GP letter, just as an opinion from a qualified specialist – such as a psychologist or a psychiatrist in cases of mental disorder – 'trumps' an opinion from a non-specialist). It is possible for an employee in such circumstances to refuse permission for the occupational health report to be shared with the employer. However, such refusal would normally make it much more reasonable for the employer to proceed with disciplinary or other action against the employee without further medical advice.

It is also important to remember that just because you think the employee is faking it, doesn't mean they are. Once you receive the occupational health report, you must take care to follow up on any recommendations, such as further assessment, or you may fail in your duty of care to the employee.

There are many conditions that may look like malingering to an employer but are actually valid mental health conditions such as factitious disorder (falsification of physical or psychological symptoms without reward), somatoform disorder (psychological distress from imagined or exaggerated symptoms), health anxiety (hypochondriasis) and dissociation (a survival response to trauma that involves zoning out, memory loss and inconsistent account giving). In order to recognise these, a specialist assessment by a clinical psychologist or a psychiatrist will be required (please see the contact details of Psychology Associates near the back of this book for advice).

A more recent and much less understood condition is long COVID, which may create symptoms that could be misinterpreted as malingering or indeed give more opportunity for someone to malinger. Again, this will require specialist medical and psychological assessment to ascertain what is going on.

Conflicting GP and occupational health reports

An occupational health report will trump a GP report. If you are faced with conflicting information about an employee's fitness to return to work, there is a clear pyramid of the way that tribunals prioritise medical evidence.

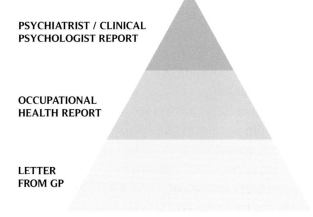

**PSYCHIATRIST / CLINICAL
PSYCHOLOGIST REPORT**

**OCCUPATIONAL
HEALTH REPORT**

**LETTER
FROM GP**

You have consultant psychiatrists and clinical psychologists at the top of the pyramid, occupational health in the middle, and at the bottom are GPs. So generally, occupational health will trump GPs and consultants will trump occupational health. Here's why.

When dealing with dismissals, a tribunal is looking at whether the employer acted reasonably. You know the test: reasonable grounds, reasonable belief, reasonable investigation, reasonable sanction. Did the employer act reasonably in all circumstances? It is very difficult, save in exceptional circumstances, to conceive of a situation where a tribunal will say that an employer acted unreasonably in relying on an occupational health report over and above a fit note or a GP report.

What about the lawyers?

If you are representing an employer, can you, as the lawyer, get access to an employee's medical records? It used to be that solicitors got access to medical records as a matter of course, but that has changed and it is now highly unusual for the lawyer to see them in employment litigation (the position is different in personal injury claims, where the lawyer still sees them as a matter of routine).

In big, high-value cases, as the respondent's lawyer, you can enter into something called a 'confidentiality club' with the claimant's lawyer. That is where you agree with the claimant's lawyer that you can look at the medical records, but not disclose them to your client (the employer), or anybody else. Your client (the employer) has got to expressly agree to this because it is a breach of the normal professional rule that you cannot withhold information from your client.

This approach gives you the ability, if you lack confidence that your occupational health expert has read the records properly, to write a letter to occupational health saying, for example, "Can you look at the entry on 14th February 2021 and see if that changes your opinion?"

If the claimant's lawyer does not agree, and it is a big enough case, you can ask a tribunal for an order that you be allowed to look at the medical records on your undertaking that you withhold them from your client (unless you go back to the tribunal and ask permission again). Many employment judges will not be familiar with this process, and it is worth seeking out case law on the point (most commonly seen in patent and trade secret litigation, for example, The Libyan Investment Authority v Société Générale SA and others [2015] EWHC 550 (QB)).

Chapter 3
Screening Tools for Anxiety and Depression

The Hospital Anxiety and Depression Scale (HADS) is one of the screening tools that GPs and occupational health use to help diagnose anxiety or depression. Other tools include the Patient Health Questionnaire (PHQ-9), the Generalised Anxiety Disorder Assessment (GAD-7), Becks Depression Inventory (BDI), Becks Anxiety Inventory (BAI) and the General Health Questionnaire (GHQ). These are also known as psychometric measures as they have undergone rigorous validity testing. They are all self-report measures and therefore rely on the honesty and insight of the person being assessed.

As an example, this is the HADS:

Continued on next page

Hospital Anxiety and Depression Scale (HADS)

Tick the box beside the reply that is closest to how
you have been feeling in the past week. Don't take too
long over you replies: your immediate is best.

D	A	
		I feel tense or 'wound up':
	3	Most of the time
	2	A lot of the time
	1	From time to time, occasionally
	0	Not at all
		I still enjoy the things I used to enjoy:
0		Definitely as much
1		Not quite so much
2		Only a little
3		Hardly at all
		I get a sort of frightened feeling as if something awful is about to happen:
	3	Very definitely and quite badly
	2	Yes, but not too badly
	1	A little, but it doesn't worry me
	0	Not at all
		I can laugh and see the funny side of things:
0		As much as I always could
1		Not quite so much now
2		Definitely not so much now
3		Not at all
		Worrying thoughts go through my mind:
	3	A great deal of the time
	2	A lot of the time
	1	From time to time, but not too often
	0	Only occasionally
		I feel cheerful:
3		Not at all
2		Not often
1		Sometimes
0		Most of the time
		I can sit at ease and feel relaxed:
	0	Definitely
	1	Usually
	2	Not Often
	3	Not at all

D	A	
		I feel as if I am slowed down:
3		Nearly all the time
2		Very often
1		Sometimes
0		Not at all
		I get a sort of frightened feeling like 'butterflies' in the stomach:
	0	Not at all
	1	Occasionally
	2	Quite Often
	3	Very Often
		I have lost interest in my appearance:
3		Definitely
2		I don't take as much care as I should
1		I may not take quite as much care
0		I take just as much care as ever
		I feel restless as I have to be on the move:
	3	Very much indeed
	2	Quite a lot
	1	Not very much
	0	Not at all
		I look forward with enjoyment to things:
0		As much as I ever did
1		Rather less than I used to
2		Definitely less than I used to
3		Hardly at all
		I get sudden feelings of panic:
	3	Very often indeed
	2	Quite often
	1	Not very often
	0	Not at all
		I can enjoy a good book or radio or TV program:
0		Often
1		Sometimes
2		Not often
3		Very seldom

Please check you have answered all the questions

Scoring:
Total score: Depression (D) _____ Anxiety (A) _____
0-7   = Normal
8-10   = Borderline abnormal (borderline case)
11-21 = Abnormal (case)

You will see each question is scored by the employee from 0 to 3, depending on how often they experienced those symptoms in the last week.

After the employee has been through all fourteen questions with their GP or occupational health provider, they will have a total score out of 21 for anxiety, and 21 for depression.

It will immediately be apparent to you that it is not difficult to generate a false impression of depression or anxiety (and let me make clear that I am not doubting these are genuine conditions that have a real and crippling effect on the lives of many, many people). All that the employee who wishes to malinger will need to do is tell the GP or occupational health practitioner that they suffer from those symptoms frequently (whereas in fact, they might only do so infrequently, or not at all).

You can access a very similar version of this test on the NHS website. It is called the 'depression and anxiety self-assessment quiz' and it has 18 questions: https://www.nhs.uk/mental-health/self-help/guides-tools-and-activities/depression-anxiety-self-assessment-quiz/ (this shortened link might be easier: go.danielbarnett.com/malingering/quiz)

These are only screening tools and should not be used in isolation to make a diagnosis. Psychological professionals insist on a thorough clinical interview and assessment to form diagnoses where these screening tools will be included as a small part of the overall assessment. Psychology Associates can be contacted to discuss these assessments and their details are at the back of this book.

So, what can you do? In Chapter 4, I identify seven factors that point to malingering, and in Chapter 5, I examine the way that clinical psychologists will detect malingerers using symptom validity testing and clinical interviewing.

Chapter 4
Seven Pointers to Malingering

Over the years that I've been practising as a barrister, I've noticed that most cases involving malingering have themes that consistently appear. There are seven of them in total, and there will usually be at least two of them present in any malingering case.

As an employer, HR professional or lawyer, you cannot 'diagnose' malingering. The relevance of these seven pointers is that if two or more of them exist, you have an objectively credible reason to suspect someone is malingering and thus a credible reason to investigate further.

That is really important to avoid an allegation of constructive dismissal. The question a tribunal will ask in a constructive dismissal claim is, "Have you acted in a way which is likely to seriously damage or destroy the relationship of trust and confidence without good cause?"

If you have sent an employee to a clinical psychologist for a report, stating, "I think this person is faking it. Can you check them out for malingering?" then you have done something likely to seriously damage or destroy the relationship between employer and employee. That will be a breach of trust and confidence, and hence constructive dismissal, unless you can demonstrate you had 'good cause' for your actions. If you can demonstrate that two or more of these seven pointers exist, you have the 'good cause' to go on to the next step and ask a clinical psychologist for direct assessment for whether somebody is malingering or not.

Please note this is just my guidance based on my many years of experience; these are not official steps/ guidelines that can be quoted in a tribunal.

1. Inconsistencies in presentation

This refers to any inconsistency between what the employee says they can and can't do and their medical records or their conduct on examination.

In Chapter 1, I explored the example of asking the employee how high they can raise their arm now and how high they could raise it before. Another example is a lack of recall of medical history. A clinical psychologist or occupational health might ask, "Have you been in good health? Have you had any previous major health problems?" And the employee might reply, "Yes, I've been in good health. I've been in fine fettle for the last 20 years." However, the GP notes could actually show something else: perhaps the employee has suffered from depression previously. That points towards the fact that they're not being honest, because you would expect them, if they are absent with stress, to remember and mention that they had been diagnosed with depression previously. It is relevant; it is the sort of thing you wouldn't withhold from a medical professional. If the employee does withhold this kind of information, it's an indicator that they are malingering. It's not conclusive on its own, but it is an indicator. It is not, without more evidence, an infallible indicator. Some genuinely mentally ill people lack insight into their own symptoms and tend to underreport them.

2. Wrongful attribution of symptoms

This is where an employee claims that all their symptoms are triggered by, say, their harassment at work. However, because of discussions at the watercooler or comments in the GP records, you know that there are other possible causes of the stress.

Common examples of other, just as likely, triggers include an employee recently having been through a divorce, or recently having suffered the bereavement of a loved one.

Anybody who is in the middle of a divorce, and who is feeling stressed, knows that the divorce is going to be a major cause of that stress. Don't forget that stress is cumulative, that is, stress at home will add to stress at work, not be separate from it. It might not be the only cause, but it is certainly going to be a significant contributor. If an employee going through a divorce visits occupational health and says, "I'm really stressed and unhappy, and it's all because Jimmy is being mean to me at work and not giving me good enough scores on my appraisals," then the employee must know there are other potential causes. By withholding that information from occupational health (or from the GP), it is an indicator that the employee is willing to exaggerate and displace responsibility. Again, it is not sufficient on its own, but it is an indicator of malingering.

Of course, if an employee is stressed and muddle-headed enough, they may genuinely attribute the sources of their stress incorrectly. A good response is a proper stress risk assessment done by HR or the employee's line manager (occupational health generally won't do these assessments; they recommend they're done by the employer who understands events and situations better). By asking the employee to list the exact stress factors and discussing each in turn, it can become clearer if they are overreacting to work issues.

A member of the HR Inner Circle gave me the example of a genuine sickness case in 2020 where one of their ex-employees had a severe mental crisis which the employee blamed entirely on work events. By doing a thorough assessment of each work stressor in turn with the employee, it became clear that most of these stressors were either minor perceived slights, unevidenced assumptions, or situations that had occurred years previously but which had become very important again in the employee's memory. Even after the risk assessment, the employee could not perceive that she was displacing responsibility for her mental health, but it helped the organisation understand where its responsibilities started and ended.

3. Covert surveillance images of other activities

I go into much more detail on this in Chapter 6, but briefly, you must treat any evidence obtained through covert surveillance with considerable caution. It will rarely be enough to prove malingering on its own, but again, it can be a factor.

There is a tendency to think you have a slam dunk case if you send out a private investigator to follow an employee who is on sick leave and obtain footage of them doing activities you think they should be unable to do. For example, you might see an employee carrying large carrier bags full of groceries home from a supermarket and think it shows that the employee hasn't got a bad back. But the employee could just respond by saying, "I was having a good day," or "My doctor told me to try and get out when I felt up to it." The same might apply if you see an employee with depression going to do some charity work or going to the theatre. The employee could say, "I was having a good day, and my doctor said it's good to get out if I can."

Another member of the HR Inner Circle gave me an example of ongoing gossip in his workplace suggesting that sick employees from a factory were moonlighting as minicab drivers. This gave great after-dinner stories, but investigation showed it was complete nonsense in almost all cases.

4. Medico-legal referral

I mentioned this briefly in Chapter 1 with regards to DSM-V and the four criteria that clinical psychologists will refer to. If an employee has been referred for a medical opinion to a clinical psychologist by a lawyer, or the employee's lawyer is in contact with your organisation, that is an indicator that what they are really after is compensation. They are not necessarily focused, or solely focused, on getting better. Again, it's a factor.

5. Not cooperating with occupational health / medical advice

This involves an employee who doesn't cooperate with a doctor or doesn't follow the prescribed treatment plan. For example, the employee might give a very fluent account of their symptoms to their GP, but be resistant, closed and avoid revealing much when talking to occupational health. If the employee is much more guarded with the employer's doctors than with their own, it is an indicator that something might be wrong.

It's rare that people who are malingering admit that they aren't taking their prescribed medication. But sometimes they slip up. Not taking medication that has been prescribed to fix the alleged injury/illness can indicate that the employee is not actually in the pain they claim to be suffering. Note, though, that there are other possible reasons why someone might not take their prescribed medication, such as unpleasant side effects. This can be explored further in an assessment interview.

6. Non-precise answers

If the employee is giving very generalised answers, such as "it hurts" or "I can't move it," but not specifying where it hurts or what particular movement they cannot make, that is another indicator for malingering.

If the employee is in pain, the more specific they can be about their illness or injury, the more likely the doctor is to be able to help them and fix the problem. It is in their interest to be specific, so not doing so is an indicator.

Here's a personal example: about 25 years ago, I dislocated my right shoulder whilst skiing. After that, it dislocated repeatedly. After ten or so dislocations, I had surgery to fix it back into place. Although my shoulder has now not dislocated in about 20 years, I have mild restricted movement; I cannot put my right arm behind my back or reach my arm out behind me. These are movements I can freely do with my left arm and which I'm sure most people can do if they are free from a similar injury. The only people that would know that they can't do this specific movement are people that have genuinely had this surgery and suffer from this injury.

So, what does that mean? Imagine I went to a doctor, complaining about having a problem with my right shoulder. The doctor might ask me, "Are there any things that you're having difficulty with?" If I reply, "Yes, lots of things," the doctor may then ask, "Do you have any problems with driving?" Now, a malingerer would most likely say, "Yes, I have problems with driving. I really struggle with driving." But someone like me, who genuinely suffers from the condition, would likely give a much more detailed answer. If I was asked that question, I would say, "I can steer without difficulty. But what I can't do is reach behind me with my right arm for my seatbelt. I have to twist around and reach for my seatbelt with my left arm." The doctor would know that is a genuine symptom. But the malingerer wouldn't, because they wouldn't have experienced it. So, when describing symptoms, malingerers speak in much more general terms. A response such as, "I really struggle with driving, doctor," is less persuasive, and it suggests a lack of detail, knowledge or cooperation.

7. Unexplained comments in medical records

Back in the 1970s and 1980s, before everything was digitised, GP records used to be written on little brown cards. When the Access to Medical Reports Act 1988 came into force, suddenly everyone could get access to their GP records. People wanted to see their cards and there would be all sorts of GP acronyms or unexplained comments. There would be things on there that people didn't understand because GPs had their own code language. You rarely see these anymore, but when you do see them, they can be quite amusing. Here are some common codes used over the years:

- NFN – normal for Norfolk

- GLM – good looking mum

- TEETH – tried everything else, try homeopathy

- TTFO – told to [you guess the word!] off

- UBI – unexplained beer injury

- LOBNH – lights on but nobody home

If your employee was told to go away (TTFO) by their GP, that is a good indicator that there is nothing wrong with them and they could be malingering. So, if you spot this, that's the second indicator.

If two or more of the seven pointers exist, you can go to the next stage of asking a clinical psychologist to undertake a more in-depth psychological assessment, as set out in Chapter 5, without the likelihood of finding yourself facing a constructive dismissal claim as a result.

Chapter 5

Psychological Assessment for Malingering

Any clinical psychologist can assess for malingering. An assessment comprises:

- Psychometric testing. The tests will vary depending on the reported symptoms, such as mental health issues, memory difficulties, head injury, etc., and will include some symptom validity testing.

- Clinical Interview. This will involve asking the employee about their symptoms and onset as well as a full psychological, social and medical history. The clinical psychologist will also ask for more detail about some of the responses on the employee's psychometrics. This helps to assess for risk and test the validity of the employee's responses.

- Medical records review. Records are analysed and cross-referenced with the information gained in interview and possible third-party accounts.

- Review of third-party information. This could include a telephone interview with a member of the family, or with a manager within the employee's work setting who has access to their personnel file.

The assessment will also look out for what is referred to as the 'magnificent seven'. These are:

1. Rare symptoms – over-reporting of symptoms that are usually very infrequent

2. Improbable symptoms – unlikely, over-dramatic or bizarre symptoms

3. Symptom combinations – psychological symptoms that do not usually occur together

4. Symptom severity – symptoms expressed as always severe, continuous or extreme

5. Indiscriminate symptom endorsement – claiming to suffer a vast array of symptoms

6. Obvious vs. subtle symptoms – focusing more on obvious well-known symptoms

7. Reported vs. observed symptoms – inconsistencies between these. Do the symptoms suddenly increase after the inconsistency has been noticed and commented upon?

Expect the assessment and report to take between 10 and 15 hours and to be charged at an hourly rate of between £120 and £150. (If you want to discuss this with a qualified clinical psychologist, contact details for Psychology Associates are provided at the back of this book.)

What is symptom validity testing?

Symptom validity testing is checking the reliability of the symptoms from which people are claiming to suffer. It is an important part of assessing whether malingering is present. There are different ways to do this within clinical assessment and different tools to use. With physical symptoms, a doctor might present a list of symptoms and ask, "Which of these symptoms are you suffering from?" Some of the symptoms on the list will be genuine symptoms you would expect for the condition the person claims to suffer from, and some of them will not.

Here's a silly, oversimplified example to explain how it works. Assume someone is suffering from a broken arm. You would expect a symptom to be a sore arm. So, the employee will say yes if asked about that symptom. But the examining doctor will also throw in some implausible symptoms by asking something like, "Does your left nostril get blocked?" That symptom has nothing to do with a broken arm, so you would expect someone genuinely suffering from a broken arm to say no. But the malingerer doesn't know what the answer is, because they are not genuinely suffering from the condition. Malingerers will get the answer wrong more frequently than the genuine sufferer. Over the course of a large data set (meaning lots and lots of similar questions), the doctor can build up a picture and tell that the person is likely to be malingering.

So, how does that work when it comes to psychological symptoms? There is no way of looking into someone's head to work out whether they are suffering from depression or stress. There are several psychometric measures designed to test symptom validity that can only be administered by clinical psychologists and psychiatrists, including the Minnesota Multiphasic Personality Inventory Test (MMPI), the Personality Assessment Inventory (PAI), the Structured Interview of Reported Symptoms (SIRS), the Structured Inventory of Malingered Symptomology (SIMS), the Paulhus Deception Scale (PDS) and the Test of Memory Malingering (TOMM).

Clinical psychologists are also trained to notice and interpret a person's presentation and non-verbal communication. This helps to inform a decision about whether someone is being truthful about their symptoms. As being untruthful generally takes up more energy than being truthful, clinical psychologists also look out for unusual or unexpected signs of fatigue.

Minnesota Multiphasic Personality Inventory Test

The Minnesota Multiphasic Inventory Test is a series of 567 yes or no questions, all of which are answered by the employee ticking boxes. Some of the questions relate to symptoms that they would genuinely have if they were suffering from depression or anxiety and some do not. The more wrong answers the employee gives (wrong in the sense that they claim to be suffering from symptoms that they shouldn't be), the more likely it is that they are malingering. The test comprises three scales: the lie scale (L), the infrequency scale (F) and the defensive scale (K).

The test was popular in the 1970s and 1980s, but it fell out of fashion for the simple reason that it returned too many false positives. (Think about it: an employee who is genuinely suffering from severe depression may not be able to concentrate for long enough to answer 567 questions accurately, so they may end up ticking answers at random and inevitably getting answers 'wrong'.)

As a result, the test was revised into a much shorter version, known as the Lees-Haley Fake Bad Scale.

Lees-Haley Fake Bad Scale

This test was created by Dr Lees-Haley, hence its name. It consists of just 43 questions taken from the Minnesota Multiphasic Personality Inventory Test, which are meant to be the most indicative. The questions are not available in the public domain (you won't find them on the Internet), and clinical psychologists who administer this test have to sign an undertaking that they will not disclose them. That is because the moment the questions are available in the public domain, they become valueless. If it was possible to look up the questions online and learn what the correct answers are, the test would be invalidated.

This remains a controversial test because although it has significantly fewer questions than the Minnesota Multiphasic Personality Inventory Test, there are still people for whom 43 questions are too many. So, it's not perfect, but it's better.

Personality Assessment Inventory

This test has gained in popularity over the MMPI as it is more contemporary, easier to administer and has high reliability and validity. It consists of 344 questions and statements, with each having a choice of severity for the employee to tick. It has to be self-administered under supervision. The results are then divided into scales for validity, clinical, treatment and interpersonal features. Within the validity scale, there are scores for the following categories:

- inconsistency (is the employee answering consistently?)

- infrequency (are they responding carelessly or randomly?)

- negative impression (are they exaggerating an unfavourable impression, or malingering?) and,

- positive impression (are they trying to present a false favourable impression?)

Paulhus Deception Scale

The Paulhus Deception Scale is a helpful self-reporting instrument because it can identify individuals who are likely to have distorted their responses on other psychometric instruments. So, it is often used concurrently with some of the measures mentioned above to indicate their validity (how likely the results on these measures are to be an accurate representation of the situation). It looks at Impression Management (the tendency for employees to inflate descriptions of themselves because of contextual factors) and Self-Deceptive Enhancement (honest inflation of self-descriptors).

You won't be able to get occupational health to administer any of these psychometric tests; you need to instruct a clinical psychologist as they have the expertise to score and interpret. Occupational health might be able to do other sorts of symptom validity testing, for example, the axial compression test, but they have to be asked to do it (they won't do it on their own initiative). In order to ask them to do it, you will generally need to show two of the seven pointers to malingering from Chapter 4 to reduce the risk of a constructive dismissal claim.

From an employer's point of view, the test is used to persuade a tribunal that dismissal on the grounds of malingering is fair, and recognised psychometrics administered as part of a psychological assessment help the employer to get past the post.

To persuade a tribunal that a dismissal for malingering is fair, you've got to show four things (it's known as the Burchell test).

First, you must show that you honestly believe the employee is guilty of malingering. This hurdle is normally pretty straightforward; if you've gone to the expense and trouble of obtaining a clinical psychologist's report, and the report supports a finding of malingering, it is highly unlikely a tribunal will think you didn't honestly believe it to be true.

Second, you must show that you undertook a reasonable investigation. Here, you will have instructed a clinical psychologist to apply the best clinical tests and interviews there are, so you are a considerable way towards satisfying this condition. You also need to have followed a fair procedure, which will include giving the employee the opportunity to comment on the medical report, holding at least one meeting and offering a right of appeal. All HR professionals will be familiar with disciplinary procedures. I address the investigation in more detail in Chapter 6.

Third, you must have reasonable grounds for your belief that the employee is malingering. Again, if, after applying robust symptom validity testing and a thorough clinical interview, a clinical psychologist has produced a report stating that the employee is malingering, that is sufficient to satisfy this condition unless there is something else putting you on notice that the psychologist might have got it wrong (in which case, further investigation is needed).

Fourth, the dismissal has to be within the range of reasonable responses (i.e., that an employer might reasonably dismiss rather than, say, just issuing a warning). A good example of this is Metroline West Ltd v Ajaj.

**Metroline West Ltd v Ajaj
(UKEAT/0185/15/RN)**

The claimant was a bus driver who suffered an accident at work. He claimed that he developed a bad back as a result. The fact that he had a bad back meant that he couldn't drive for 40 hours a week; he was limited to driving for a few hours a day. But he claimed he couldn't drive at all and went on long-term sick. When it was discovered that he had exaggerated his symptoms to occupational health, he was dismissed for gross misconduct.

He brought a claim in the employment tribunal. The employment tribunal held the claimant was unfairly dismissed because the employer didn't look at what he actually could do. The tribunal criticised the employer for not offering the claimant a role for the three or four hours' work he could do each day. But the Employment Appeal Tribunal overturned that approach. It held that if an employee fakes illness or exaggerates their symptoms, that will normally amount to gross misconduct. Since gross misconduct goes to the root of the employment contract, it will normally be reasonable to dismiss the employee without notice.

One member of the HR Inner Circle (more information about the HR Inner Circle at the back of this book) told me that she employed a teacher who was off sick for around 12 months following a hip replacement, shoulder replacement, and various other ailments. The teacher told the school that he could not lift his arm up to write on the whiteboard and that he could not possibly return until he was a lot better.

The school suspected he was malingering and that he was providing private tuition whilst on paid sick leave. The school decided (after seeking legal advice) to use covert surveillance. It had fairly convincing footage covering four days of normal activity, and then, on day five, the teacher was filmed lifting the bonnet of his wife's broken-down car right up and also pushing the car.

When the school met the teacher after obtaining the footage (before they showed it to him), the teacher claimed he had not been able to get out of the house.

After a protracted disciplinary hearing, the teacher was dismissed. He appealed, and then took the school to an employment tribunal. He lost. The judge decided that the teacher had been fairly dismissed and that the school was within its rights to use covert surveillance because it had no other reasonable way of eliciting the truth as the teacher had been so deceitful during the process.

Chapter 6
Investigating Suspected Malingering

If you strongly suspect an employee of malingering, it is only natural to want to catch them out. Whether this is looking at photos they've posted on Facebook of their activities or hiring a private investigator to follow the employee. What is reasonable? Will it be reasonable – from an unfair dismissal perspective – to rely on evidence obtained by covert surveillance?

It can be, yes, as long as you are not treating the employee unfairly in the process, and it's only done in exceptional circumstances. One important rule is to be very clear about the evidence you're looking for. Surveillance (or monitoring) in this context should never be used as a 'let's see what we can find' exercise. Make sure that you have a specific allegation firmly in mind. You must use the evidence responsibly, not only in line with rules on data processing but also when interpreting what it means for the particular employee involved.

Social media

Particular care needs to be taken where social media is concerned. More and more disciplinary issues are resulting from employees' ill-advised posts, and it is unrealistic for an employer to avoid coming across, or turn a blind eye to, incriminating evidence on an employee's public social media accounts.

There are data protection issues to consider, however. A social media post that identifies the employee counts as personal data under the GDPR, even if it is freely available for anyone to see. You would need a lawful basis for processing (i.e., storing or using) that information. Employee consent would be ideal, but that can be difficult to establish, and so 'legitimate interests' is normally the most appropriate basis. You would need to be confident that processing the data is necessary for your legitimate interests and that there is no good reason to protect the employee's personal data – think about the employee's fundamental rights and freedoms – that overrides those legitimate interests. You will find a lot more about data protection in Book 2 in the Employment Law Library, GDPR for HR Professionals, which you can find on Amazon or at go.danielbarnett.com/books/gdpr.

These issues should all be addressed before putting the information you have discovered to the employee, asking for an explanation and relying on that evidence against them if necessary. Remember to comply with your social media and data protection policies, and your privacy notice. Also bear in mind that as well as having a lawful basis to process data, your processing must be fair and transparent.

In very extreme (and idiotic!) circumstances, you may come across an employee who forgets they are friends with their colleagues or employer on Facebook and posts something like, "Can't believe I got away with this! I skived off work and went to the football!" But that is very unusual.

Nowadays, people tend to be more astute about their social media use, and it will be rare to see something so brazen. But if you do, it is certainly enough to warrant an investigation, as taken at face value, it appears the employee is being dishonest about their illness/injury and therefore malingering.

A member of the HR Inner Circle told me the story of a manager giving a briefing, part of which was to explain that a particular team member was off sick. A football match was playing on TV in the background. Eventually, one of the other team members interrupted the manager to say, "I think you need to look behind you." And there was the missing colleague, right as rain, caught on camera amongst the crowd at the match!

Much more common is a situation like this: an employee is off sick and describes their symptoms as not being able to do anything and not being able to get out of bed. But then you see on Facebook that they have gone on holiday. Is that enough for an allegation of malingering?

It certainly sets up a rebuttable presumption, but you would want something more. First of all, that information should be checked. When was the photo taken and when was it posted? Is it definitely them?

Even if you can verify the photo, you would still want something more because sometimes, an employee saying they can't get out of bed doesn't literally mean they can't get out of bed. A GP may very well say to somebody, "Do what you can. See if you can play a round of golf or see if you can go to the seaside for a couple of days. It would be really good for your mental health to get away from your home situation for a day." Sometimes, an employee won't be fit enough to attend work but will be fit enough to do other activities that you might not expect them to be able to do.

So, the mere act of going on holiday does not prove malingering, but it is certainly a factor. As I've set out in Chapter 4, if you identify several of these factors, then together they build up a picture of malingering.

To put it another way, there's a world of difference between being fit enough to work and being fit enough to smile in a photograph and look happy. Just because someone manages the latter does not show they can manage the former, and tribunals are reluctant to accept this sort of thing as evidence of malingering unless it is overwhelmingly one-sided and not capable of any more innocuous explanation. Despite what you, as an employer, may think, it rarely is.

Colleague as a witness

A colleague might tell you that they saw the sick employee at the football, "and she looked fine," or say something like, "It's odd that he posted a selfie from Center Parcs when he hadn't managed to make it into work." Always remember, of course, that some illnesses cannot be seen.

As tempting as it may be to decide there and then to haul the absent employee over the coals, step back. You should not assume that something a colleague reports to you is right, or that it is a true reflection of the situation. The colleague may have been mistaken in what they saw or heard. Worse, they may have an ulterior motive. See if you can verify the information and establish whether or not there is some sort of issue between the two employees that could cast doubt on the veracity of what you have been told. That said, if you investigate properly, there is no reason why the colleague's evidence can't be used.

Covert surveillance

What about trying to catch a malingering employee red-handed? While covert surveillance is not automatically the wrong thing to do, it should only be used in exceptional cases. It needs to be proportionate (is there a less intrusive way of getting the information?) and there must be a specific focus rather than a general search for something that implicates the employee. It may be wise to check that the investigator is a member of a recognised trade association before engaging them. In Appendix II, you can read the 'covert monitoring' section of the Employment Practices Code, published by the Information Commissioner's Office.

Let's say, for example, you have an employee who has been off work with a chronic shoulder injury, but whom you are told has been caught on film playing tennis with moderate gusto. Most employers would assume the employee is taking them for a ride. But that's not a safe assumption to make. The safe thing to do would be to take that evidence and show it to a suitably qualified medical professional. I realise it might sound like overkill – especially where the employee's duplicity could not be more brazen – but a tribunal will expect that, and failure to do so is likely to make a dismissal unfair (assuming the employee has the two years' qualifying service required to claim unfair dismissal).

Sometimes, it will be more nuanced. What if you have an employee who claimed he hurt his back at work so badly he could hardly walk, yet CCTV showed him walking around normally shortly afterwards? He has been on sick leave for four months and a recent MRI shows no new injury. Is this sufficient to say the employee is malingering?

No. It may be an indicator of malingering, but you would need to investigate further. Sometimes, somebody who injures their back does get up and walk around afterwards, then their back gets worse and worse over the coming hours and days. It's common, particularly with soft tissue injuries, as opposed to bone injuries. If it was a soft tissue lower back injury, which can last for years, there could be no immediate symptoms and then the pain might increase over the following 24-72 hours. In this situation, you would want to go to a consultant orthopaedic surgeon and ask them to perform symptom validity testing (I gave the example in Chapter 5 of the axial compression test).

So, the lesson in this sort of situation is to get an appropriate medical professional to look at the footage and give their opinion on its significance. The courts are unlikely to look favourably on an employer who thinks they know best.

I explored constructive dismissal (in Chapter 4) in the context of undermining trust and confidence by referring an employee to a medical expert to investigate malingering. Constructive dismissal is also a risk when carrying out covert surveillance. An employee could resign, claiming breach of trust and confidence on discovery that their employer has been covertly surveilling them. The tribunal would need to weigh up the employer's reason for the covert recording against the employee's right to privacy under Article 8 of the European Convention on Human Rights.

So, is it a breach of the employee's privacy? Generally, tribunals will express disapproval at the way the evidence was obtained but will allow it as the probative value outweighs the public interest in discouraging covert surveillance. In my experience, that is what tribunals do when the employer is in the private sector. It can be different for the public sector.

Dismissal for gross misconduct

If you are confident that an employee is malingering, and you have evidence to back that up, then provided that you follow a proper and fair procedure, you should be safe to dismiss for gross misconduct. It is not a capability dismissal, it is a conduct dismissal; you are dismissing them for lying about their illness, not for the absence itself.

But it is rarely that straightforward. I have been asked before what should be done if an employee who is suspected of malingering is persistently refusing to attend a welfare meeting or occupational health meeting. All you can do in that situation is act on the information you have in your possession. The best evidence is symptom validity testing, which I explored in Chapter 5, but if an employee refuses to go for those tests, if they refuse to go to occupational health, well, what do you have? You have an employee who is off work and who is refusing to cooperate.

Remember the seven pointers to malingering in Chapter 4? Failure to cooperate is pointer number six. In that situation, you are normally going to be okay embarking on a disciplinary for malingering because you've got at least two pointers to malingering (i.e., whatever triggered your suspicion in the first place, plus the employee's refusal to cooperate with medical examination). Once you start a disciplinary process, you should give the employee another chance to get the medical evidence. And if they continue to refuse, you are entitled to take that refusal into account as behaviour supporting your suspicion that they are malingering.

These are the steps you should follow for a fair dismissal on grounds of gross misconduct:

1. Carry out a thorough investigation. For suspected malingering, this will include obtaining medical evidence as set out in earlier chapters.

2. Write to the employee setting out the allegation of malingering and inviting them to a disciplinary meeting. The letter should include:

   a. full details of the allegations

b. any evidence that is being relied upon

c. details of where the employee can access the disciplinary policy

d. a reminder of the employee's right to be accompanied

e. details of the potential sanctions the employee might face

3. At the meeting, you should set out the allegations in full, go through the evidence and ensure someone is minuting the meeting. Give the employee the opportunity to respond to the allegations, ask questions and provide their own evidence or witnesses (with notice).

4. At the end of the meeting, ask the employee, "Do you think you have had a fair hearing?" If they say yes, great, you're covered. If they say no, you have a chance to rectify whatever it is they are unhappy with. Better then, than a year down the line during a tribunal hearing.

5. Also, at the end of the meeting, ask the employee whether they have anything to add. That closes down a potential argument for them at a tribunal that you didn't give them the chance to add an important piece of information that might have had a bearing on your decision.

6. Do not tell the employee your decision at the meeting. Rather, tell them that you will write to them with the outcome, and give them some idea of the timescale. If no further investigation is required, this should normally be within 48 hours. If further investigation is needed, tell them what further investigations you are planning to carry out and when you expect to be in a decision to write to them with a decision. It's fine if the timetable slips, as long as you keep them informed by writing, explaining the delay, and giving a new date by which you will conclude your investigations and reach a decision. But try not to let this second deadline slip or you could run into difficulties at a tribunal for taking unreasonably long to deal with the process.

7. Inform the employee of the outcome in writing, including their right to appeal.

If you follow these steps and carry out a reasonable investigation (including obtaining medical evidence), and you have reasonable grounds for your belief in guilt (normally based on the medical evidence), you are unlikely to face a claim of unfair dismissal.

Appendix I
Letter Informing an Employee they are the Subject of an Investigation

Date ....

Dear ....

I am writing to inform you that [organisation] has decided it is necessary to conduct an investigation into your actions in relation to:

[Summarise details of each issue being investigated in a bulleted list]

The person in charge of the investigation will be *[name of investigator]*.

The aim of the investigation is to establish the facts of the matter by gathering as many relevant facts, and as much information, as possible. It is currently expected that the investigation will be completed by *[date]*.

The investigator may ask you to attend an investigation meeting where you can explain your version of events.

Once the investigation has been completed, you will be informed in writing of its outcome. If it is found that there is a case to answer, you will be invited to attend a formal disciplinary hearing at which you can be accompanied by a workplace colleague or a trade union official.

In the meantime, should you have any information that might be of assistance to the investigation or wish to discuss anything, please do not hesitate to contact *[name of investigator/line manager/HR department]*. Their contact details are *[telephone number, email address]*.

To ensure that the investigation can be conducted as fairly as possible, we ask that you keep the matter confidential. Any breach of confidentiality may be considered to be a disciplinary matter in its own right.

Please note that you should continue to attend work while the investigation takes place *[amend if suspension of the employee is necessary or if they remain off sick]*.

Yours sincerely

Signed ....

Appendix II
The Employment Practices Code (Extract)

Part 3: Monitoring at Work

3.4. Covert monitoring

Covert monitoring means monitoring carried out in a manner calculated to ensure those subject to it are unaware that it is taking place. This sub-section is largely directed at covert video or audio monitoring, but will also be relevant where electronic communications are monitored when workers would not expect it.

3.4.1 Senior management should normally authorise any covert monitoring. They should satisfy themselves that there are grounds for suspecting criminal activity or equivalent malpractice and that notifying individuals about the monitoring would prejudice its prevention or detection.

Key points and possible actions

- Covert monitoring should not normally be considered. It will be rare for covert monitoring of workers to be justified. It should therefore only be used in exceptional circumstances.

3.4.2 Ensure that any covert monitoring is strictly targeted at obtaining evidence within a set timeframe and that the covert monitoring does not continue after the investigation is complete.

Key points and possible actions

- Deploy covert monitoring only as part of a specific investigation and cease once the investigation has been completed.

3.4.3 Do not use covert audio or video monitoring in areas which workers would genuinely and reasonably expect to be private.

Key points and possible actions

- If embarking on covert monitoring with audio or video equipment, ensure that this is not used in places such as toilets or private offices.

- There may be exceptions to this in cases of suspicion of serious crime but there should be an intention to involve the police.

3.4.4 If a private investigator is employed to collect information on workers covertly, make sure there is a contract in place that requires the private investigator to only collect information in a way that satisfies the employer's obligations under the Act [note: this refers to the Data Protection Act 2018].

Key points and possible actions

- Check any arrangements for employing private investigators to ensure your contracts with them impose requirements on the investigator to only collect and use information on workers in accordance with your instructions and to keep the information secure.

3.4.5 Ensure that information obtained through covert monitoring is used only for the prevention or detection of criminal activity or equivalent malpractice. Disregard and, where feasible, delete other information collected in the course of monitoring unless it reveals information that no employer could reasonably be expected to ignore.

Key points and possible actions

- In a covert monitoring exercise, limit the number of people involved in the investigation.

- Prior to the investigation, set up clear rules limiting the disclosure and access to information obtained.

- If information is revealed in the course of covert monitoring that is tangential to the original investigation, delete it from the records unless it concerns other criminal activity or equivalent malpractice.

Also by
Daniel Barnett

Available on Amazon
or visit
go.danielbarnett.com/books

JOIN DANIEL EVERY SATURDAY EVENING AT
9PM WHEN HE PRESENTS THE ALL-NEW

LBC LEGAL HOUR

— OR CATCH UP VIA THE GLOBAL PLAYER,
AT bit.ly/lbclegalhour

SATURDAYS, 9PM

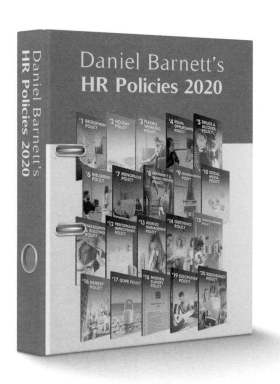

I have updated my 20 Employment Law Policies for small businesses.

If you are an HR professional, they are perfect for incorporating into a staff handbook. If you are a solicitor, they come with a licence for you to resell them or give them away for free to clients.

HR INNER CIRCLE

"The HR Inner Circle has improved my life amazingly, mainly because it means I have to spend less time researching and more time and more time actually doing the work I'm paid for."

Sue Whittle, Employment & Safety Advice LTD

Join to gain access to the monthly HR Inner Circular magazine

jam-packed with amazing information for ambitious HR professionals

What do you get?

1 Monthly live online 'Ask Me Anything' sessions: each month, we host an online video webinar, when you can share your HR problems and ask Daniel anything about employment law. You'll also receive a recording and a transcript each month, so you have a permanent record of the session even if you cannot be there.

DANIEL BARNETT'S
HR INNER CIRCLE

Please ask your questions now:
1. click 'Raise Hand'; or,
2. type it into the Questions box

"Daniel Barnett is an inspirational, walking and talking 'how to understand mind-boggling employment law handbook!"

Ellie King, HR Manager, RWE Technology

2 A specially recorded audio seminar every month, with HR shortcuts and workarounds you can't get anywhere else.

WWW.HRINNERCIRCLE.CO.UK

3   The monthly Inner Circular magazine, jam-packed with valuable information for ambitious HR professionals.

4   Access to Daniel's exclusive, private, invitation-only online Inner Circle group, where you get to discuss HR problems with other smart, ambitious professionals and download precedents and policies they have shared.

"It's the support and help that you get, the reassurance that you're talking to people who know what they're talking about rather than people just randomly giving information."

Nicky Jolley, HR2DAY LTD

5   Access to the exclusive HR Inner Circle website which includes a back-catalogue of all the HRIC resources since the launch in 2015.

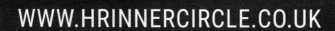

WWW.HRINNERCIRCLE.CO.UK

If you are looking for a forum to discuss confidential issues that need prompt employment law advice, then the HR Inner Circle is definitely for you. In addition it offers other tools to help and support. The Facebook group is full of information and solutions to scenarios — invaluable for HR professionals.

- **Sheena Doyle**, Managing Director, The Really Useful HR Company Ltd

It's a forum where you're not afraid to ask stupid questions, even though I'm not usually afraid of doing that. The sheer variety of experience and skillsets ensures there is always an informed discussion. JOIN NOW!!

- **Jon Dews**, HR & Business Partner, Majestic 12 Ltd

If you are looking for a steady stream of thorough, pragmatic, and easily-digestible employment law advice, the HR Inner Circle is a great place to be.

- **Susi O'Brien**, Senior Manager HR, The Action Group

The regular updates are invaluable to not only me, but also my team. We find that they are presented in an easy to digest format and aren't too 'legalistic'.

- **Donna Negus**, Sekoya Specialist Employment Services

WWW.HRINNERCIRCLE.CO.UK

There aren't many other employment law advice services where you get direct access to an employment law barrister at a realistic price. Join the HR Inner Circle now – you won't regret it.

- **Kirsten Cluer**, Owner of Cluer HR, HR Consultancy

I like being able to use the HR Inner Circle Facebook group to ask other members for a second opinion, or for ideas when I get stuck with solving a tricky situation. There's usually someone who has come across the situation before.

- **Helen Astill**, Managing Director, Cherington HR Ltd

When I transitioned from big employers to an SME, I didn't realise how much I would miss having peers to kick ideas around. If you haven't got an internal network, you've got to build an external one. I got so much out of the discussion at an Inner Circle meetup recently and I look forward to getting the Inner Circular.

- **Elizabeth Divver**, Group HR Director, The Big Issue Group

Sign now! The monthly Q & A sessions are invaluable, the magazine is packed full of helpful info, you get lots of goodies and the Facebook page is really informative and a useful sounding board.

- **Caroline Hitchen**, Consultant, Caroline Neal Employment Law

Being a member of HR Inner Circle is one of the best sources of HR information and advice, and receiving the monthly audio seminars and magazines is extremely helpful and interesting. I can't recommend becoming a member highly enough. There is a private Facebook group which is great for asking other members advice and sharing knowledge and experiences. I have also recently attended one of the meetups that is organised by Daniel Barnett, and it was good to meet other members (and of course Daniel) in a more social setting. It was also a good opportunity to ask any questions you wanted and being able to get advice or support as to how they would deal with whatever you ask.

- **Tracey Seymour**, HR Manager (Head of Dept), Kumon Europe & Africa Ltd

The help and advice from other HR professionals on Facebook is really valuable, and quick. All the team enjoy the audio seminars and magazines for updates on current issues.

- **Catherine Larke**, Director | myHRdept.co.uk

WWW.HRINNERCIRCLE.CO.UK

For me it's a no brainer. We have a lot of really good contributors in the HR Inner Circle and it's more than a discussion forum and invaluable source of information. When combined with the magazine, the audio seminars and events, it is a complete service especially with Daniel's legal expertise always on hand.

- **Elizabeth Ince**, Self employed HR Consultant

Just join! It is invaluable with the resources you have at hand by joining the HR Inner Circle. Especially the Facebook Group where you can get advice or a different point of view that you may not have previously considered, outside of normal working hours which is very useful. Live Q&A's too.

- **Diana Wilks**, HR Manager, Go South Coast Ltd

HR can be complex because each and every issue will have its own set of individual circumstances. Being in the HR Inner Circle enables you to bounce ideas around and make sure you are considering every angle and aspect, knowing your HR Inner Circle partners will have had a similar experience to share.

- **Pam Rogerson**, HR Director, ELAS Group

Psychology Associates

Psychology Associates have experts to help businesses perform better. We can deliver:

▶ Gold standard Mental Health and fitness to work assessments and reports

▶ Staff training in mental health and how to improve workplace well-being

▶ Consultation in recruitment to help get the right person for the job

▶ Individual and effective evidence-based therapy

▶ Support for managers to help implement organisational change

Please contact Psychology Associates to arrange a free consultation with Dr Kerry Davison (HCPC Registered Consultant Clinical Psychologist and Clinical Director) to discuss your enquiry.

0300 303 5233
enquiry@psychologyassociates.org.uk
www.psychologyassociates.org.uk